EDUCAT

On Your
Plate

Vegetables

Honor Head

W

FRANKLIN WATTS

LONDON • SYDNEY

First published in 2007 by Franklin Watts

Franklin Watts
338 Euston Road, London NW1 3BH

Franklin Watts Australia
Level 17/207 Kent Street, Sydney, NSW 2000

Copyright © Franklin Watts 2007

Created by Taglines
Design: Sumit Charles; Harleen Mehta, Q2A Media
Picture research: Pritika Ghura, Q2A Media

ISBN: 978 0 7496 7630 8

Dewey classification: 641.3'5

A CIP catalogue for this book is available from the British Library.

Picture credits
t=top b=bottom c=centre l=left r=right m=middle

Cover Images: Shutterstock and Dreamstime.
Disorderly | Dreamstime.com: 4, Shanta Giddens/ Shutterstock: 5, Agphotographer/ Shutterstock: 6t, Tom Mc Nemar/ Shutterstock:
6bl, Felinda | Dreamstime.com: 6br, content, John Clines/ Shutterstock: 7, Danny E Hooks/ Shutterstock and Steve Degenhardt/
Shutterstock: 8bl, Robert Redelowski/ Shutterstock: 8bc, Winterstorm | Dreamstime.com: 8br, Joe Gough/ Shutterstock: 9, Peter
Hansen/ Shutterstock: 10, DUSAN ZIDAR/ Shutterstock: 11, Kippy Lanker/ Shutterstock: 12, Paul Cowan/ Shutterstock: 13, Ramon
grosso dolarea / Shutterstock: 14, bora ucak/ Shutterstock: 15, Harris Shiffman/ Shutterstock: 16, Donald Gruener/ Istockphoto: 17,
Q2A Media: 18, Paul Cowan/ Shutterstock: 19, hugo chang/ Istockphoto: 20, Agphotographer/ Shutterstock: 21.

Printed in China

Franklin Watts is a division of Hachette Children's Books,
an Hachette Livre UK company.

Contents

What is a vegetable?

Carrots are the root part of the plant.

Vegetables are plants that are grown and used for food.

All vegetables are very good for you. You should eat some every day.

Munching on a crunchy raw carrot keeps your teeth strong.

Cabbage

Most cabbages have big leaves that make a round shape.

white cabbage

leaves

red cabbage

Savoy cabbage

 Different cabbages have different flavours.

Eating cabbage helps
your body to fight
off colds.

Raw cabbage
sliced with
carrots makes
a side dish
called coleslaw.

Potatoes

Potatoes grow in the ground. To cook potatoes, you often need to peel off the skin.

skin

uncooked potatoes

mashed potato

chips

 Potatoes can be mashed, baked, roasted or made into chips.

A jacket potato is cooked in the oven with the skin on.

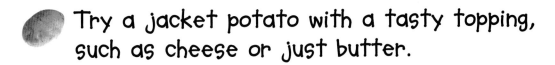 Try a jacket potato with a tasty topping, such as cheese or just butter.

Leeks

The green leaves of the leek grow above the ground.

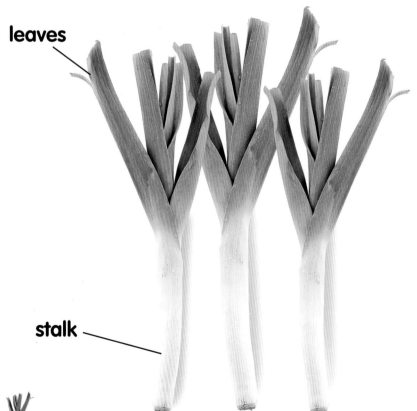

leaves

stalk

 You can eat the white stalk and green leaves.

Leeks can be steamed, fried, baked in the oven or chopped up in soups and stews.

 Leeks add flavour to warming soups.

Sprouts

Brussels sprouts grow above the ground on long, thick stalks.

stalk

 Sprouts look like mini cabbages.

Sprouts are delicious with roast turkey or chicken.

sprouts

You eat sprouts mainly during the winter.

Spinach

Spinach is a plant that has small flowers and big, green leaves.

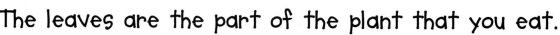

The leaves are the part of the plant that you eat.

Eating spinach makes you strong. You can eat it cooked or raw in salads.

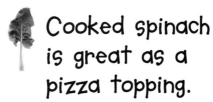

Cooked spinach is great as a pizza topping.

15

Peas

Peas grow in a pod.
The pods grow on a bush.

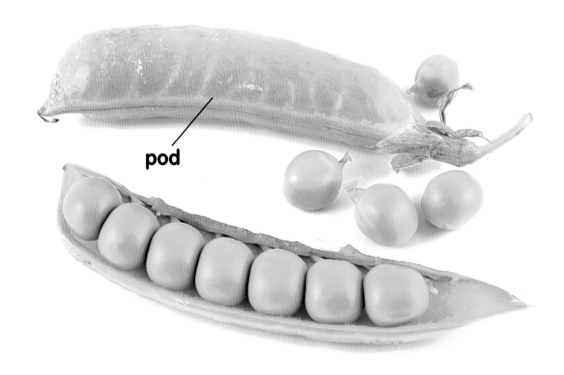

pod

  The pod is split open and the peas are taken out.

Fresh, frozen or tinned peas
are good for you.

Peas have to be cooked
before you eat them.

Broccoli

Broccoli is one of the best vegetables you can eat to keep your body healthy.

flower

leaf

stalk

 You can eat the broccoli flower, stalk and leaves.

Broccoli is usually cut into small pieces called florets.

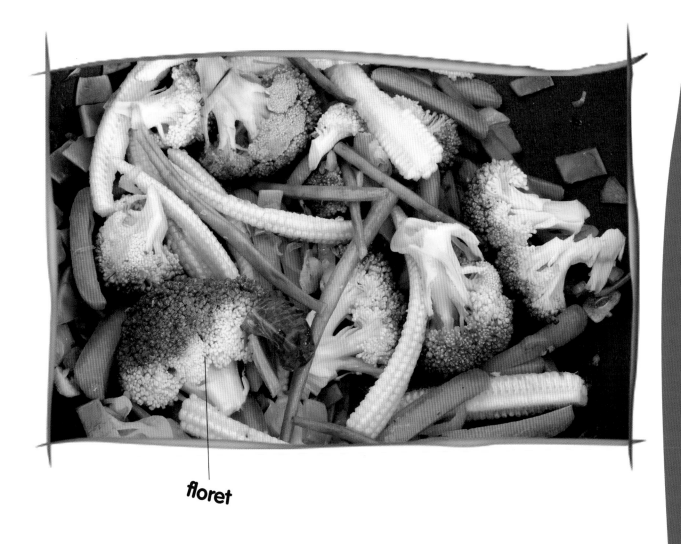

floret

 Try broccoli florets cooked in a stir fry.

Aubergine

Aubergines have a shiny purple skin. They are smooth and soft.

 You can eat the skin of the aubergine.

Aubergines are used in many different dishes around the world.

 Slices of aubergine taste good grilled or fried.

Things to do

Choose a potato

Which of these dishes are made from potatoes?
Can you name them?

Colour mix-up

Name the vegetables that are the right colour.
What colour should the others be?

Shopping basket

Can you recognise what is in this shopping basket from these descriptions?

a) I am crunchy and orange.
b) I have big leaves.
c) I grow in a pod.
d) I can be made into chips.

23

Glossary

raw
When a food is not cooked.

root
The part of the plant that grows under the ground.

stew
A hot cooked dish of lots of different vegetables or meat and vegetables.

stir fry
When lots of chopped vegetables and meat are mixed together and fried quickly in a hot pan.

Index